Modern Selling Techniques:

Mastering the Art of Sales in the Digital Age

BY

SIMEON FAVOUR

Table Of Content Introduction

Welcome to the Future of Sales!

In a world where markets are constantly evolving, and customer behaviors are rapidly changing, traditional sales techniques no longer guarantee success. To thrive in this dynamic landscape, you need to adapt and embrace the power of modern selling techniques.

In this comprehensive guide, we will take you on a journey through the cutting-edge strategies and tactics that define modern selling. Whether you're a seasoned sales professional looking to level up your game or someone just starting their sales career, this book is your roadmap to mastering the art of selling in the 21st century.

- Emerging Trends and Technologies
- Preparing for the Sales Landscape of Tomorrow
- Continuous Learning and Adaptation

Conclusion

Acknowledgments

Chapter 1: The Evolution of Sales

- The Shift from Traditional to Modern Selling
- Understanding the Modern Buyer
- The Digital Transformation of Sales

The Evolution of Sales

Sales, as a profession, has undergone a remarkable transformation throughout history. What was once a straightforward exchange of goods or services has evolved into a complex and dynamic field. This chapter explores the journey of sales, tracing its evolution from traditional methods to the modern, digitally driven landscape we know today.

The Historical Roots of Sales

Sales, in some form, has been an integral part of human society for millennia. From ancient marketplaces to the door-to-door salesmen of the 20th century, the act of selling has always been about connecting products or services with those who need them.

1. ***Barter and Trade***: In ancient times, people engaged in barter systems, swapping goods they had for items they needed. This basic form of exchange laid the foundation for future sales transactions.

2. ***Marketplaces and Bazaars***: The emergence of marketplaces and bazaars brought sellers and buyers together in centralized locations. These gatherings became hubs for commerce and the exchange of goods.

3. ***The Rise of Retail***: As societies grew more complex, permanent retail establishments began to appear. From medieval shops to department stores, retail introduced a new level of convenience for buyers.

**The Limitations of Traditional Sales**

While traditional sales methods served their purpose, they had inherent limitations:

1. _**Limited Reach**_: Traditional sales were often confined to local or regional markets, limiting the potential customer base.

2. _**Information Asymmetry:**_ Sellers held most of the information about products, leaving buyers at a disadvantage.

3. _**High Pressure:**_ Some traditional sales techniques relied on high-pressure tactics, which could alienate customers.

The Catalysts for Change

Several factors sparked the transition from traditional to modern sales methods:

1. ***Information Accessibility***: The internet and digital technology democratized information, giving buyers unprecedented access to product details and reviews.

2. ***Changing Buyer Behavior***: Modern consumers are more informed, discerning, and independent in their purchasing decisions.

3. ***Globalization***: The ability to conduct business on a global scale opened up new opportunities and challenges for sales professionals.

The Digital Transformation of Sales

The digital age ushered in a new era of sales:

1. ***E-Commerce***: Online shopping platforms revolutionized the way goods are bought and sold, making it possible to reach a global audience.

2. _**Data-Driven Insights**_: Sales professionals now have access to vast amounts of data, enabling them to understand customer behavior and preferences better.

3. _**Automation and AI:**_ Sales automation tools and artificial intelligence have streamlined processes and improved efficiency.

4. _**Social Selling**_: Social media platforms have become valuable tools for salespeople to connect with prospects and build relationships.

The Shift from Traditional to Modern Selling

The transition from traditional to modern selling represents a pivotal moment in the history of sales. This shift has redefined the way businesses connect with customers, engage in transactions, and build lasting relationships. In this section, we will explore the profound changes that have reshaped the sales landscape and the factors driving this transformation.

1.1 Understanding Traditional Selling

Traditional selling refers to age-old sales methods that were prevalent before the digital age. It was characterized by:

1. *In-Person Transactions*: Salespeople typically engaged with customers face-to-face, whether in stores, at marketplaces, or during door-to-door sales.

2. *Limited Access to Information*: Buyers had limited access to information about products and relied heavily on salespeople for details and recommendations.

3. *High-Pressure Tactics*: Some traditional sales techniques involve pressuring customers into making quick decisions.

4. *__Local and Regional Markets__*: Traditional selling was often confined to local or regional markets.

1.2 The Limitations of Traditional Selling

Traditional selling methods had inherent limitations:

1. *__Geographic Constraints__*: Sales were limited to specific geographical areas, making it challenging to reach a broader customer base.

2. *__Information Asymmetry__*: Salespeople held most of the information about products, leading to a power imbalance.

3. *__Customer Skepticism__*: High-pressure sales tactics and a lack of transparency led to customer skepticism and mistrust.

1.3 Catalysts for the Shift to Modern Selling

Several catalysts triggered the transition from traditional to modern selling:

1. *Information Accessibility*: The internet and digital technology made information readily available to consumers. Buyers could research products, read reviews, and compare prices with ease.

2. *Changing Buyer Behavior*: Modern consumers became more informed and independent in their decision-making. They no longer relied solely on salespeople for information.

3. *Globalization*: The digital world opened up global markets, enabling businesses to reach customers worldwide.

4. *Advancements in Technology*: Sales automation tools, customer relationship management (CRM) systems, and artificial intelligence transformed sales processes.

5. _E-Commerce_: Online shopping platforms revolutionized the way goods and services are bought and sold, offering a convenient and accessible shopping experience.

Understanding the Modern Buyer

In the digital age, the landscape of sales has been transformed by the emergence of the modern buyer. To succeed in modern selling, it's crucial to gain a deep understanding of the characteristics, behaviors, and expectations of this new breed of consumers. In this section, we will delve into the intricacies of the modern buyer, providing insights that will empower you to connect with and serve them effectively.

1.1 Characteristics of the Modern Buyer

Modern buyers are distinct in several ways:

1. _**Informed and Empowered**_: Modern buyers have access to a wealth of

information at their fingertips, enabling them to research products and services extensively before making a purchase decision.

2. *Tech-Savvy*: They are comfortable with technology and often engage with businesses through digital channels, including websites, social media, and mobile apps.

3. *Independent Decision-Makers*: Modern buyers are less reliant on salespeople for information. They prefer to explore options independently and make informed decisions.

4. *Skeptical and Discerning*: Due to the abundance of choices and information, modern buyers tend to be more discerning and skeptical. They seek authentic, transparent interactions with businesses.

5. _**Value-Oriented**_: While price remains a factor, modern buyers prioritize value. They want products and services that meet their needs and deliver tangible benefits.

1.2 The Buyer's Journey

Understanding the modern buyer entails recognizing the stages of the buyer's journey:

1. _**Awareness**_: At this stage, buyers identify a problem or need. They start researching potential solutions.

2. _**Consideration**_: In this phase, buyers evaluate different options, compare features, and assess value.

3. _**Decision**_: The decision stage involves selecting a specific product or service provider and making the purchase.

4. _**Post-Purchase**_: The relationship doesn't end with the sale. Modern buyers expect

ongoing support, excellent customer service, and a positive post-purchase experience.

1.3 The Importance of Customer-Centricity

To effectively engage with modern buyers, businesses must adopt a customer-centric approach:

1. *Personalization*: Tailoring interactions and offers to individual preferences and needs.

2. *Transparency*: Providing clear and honest information about products, pricing, and policies.

3. *Engagement*: Creating meaningful and authentic connections with buyers through various touchpoints.

4. ***Responsive Support:*** Offering prompt and helpful customer support throughout the entire customer journey.

5. ***Feedback Integration***: Listening to customer feedback and using it to improve products and services.

The Digital Transformation of Sales

The digital transformation of sales represents a monumental shift in how businesses connect with customers, conduct transactions, and optimize their operations. In this section, we will delve into the profound impact of digital technology on the sales landscape, exploring the key elements of this transformation and its implications for modern selling.

1.1 E-Commerce Revolution

One of the most noticeable aspects of the digital transformation is the rise of e-commerce. E-commerce has revolutionized how goods and services are bought and sold, bringing about significant changes:

1. *Global Reach*: E-commerce platforms enable businesses to reach a global audience, transcending geographical boundaries.

2. *Convenience*: Customers can shop online 24/7, making purchases at their convenience.

3. *Diverse Marketplaces*: Online marketplaces like Amazon, eBay, and Alibaba provide platforms for businesses to showcase and sell their products.

4. *Data-Driven Insights*: E-commerce generates vast amounts of data, allowing businesses to gain insights into customer behavior, preferences, and trends.

1.2 Sales Automation and CRM

Sales automation tools and Customer Relationship Management (CRM) systems have streamlined sales processes:

1. *Efficiency*: Sales automation reduces manual tasks, enabling sales teams to focus on high-value activities like building relationships and closing deals.

2. *Lead Management*: CRMs help businesses track and manage leads, ensuring no potential opportunity falls through the cracks.

3. *Data Analytics*: CRM systems provide valuable data and analytics to enhance decision-making and customer interactions.

1.3 Artificial Intelligence (AI) and Machine Learning

AI and machine learning technologies have revolutionized sales in several ways:

1. *<u>Predictive Analytics</u>*: AI can predict customer behavior and preferences, helping businesses tailor their sales and marketing strategies.

2. *<u>Chatbots</u>*: Chatbots provide instant customer support, answer inquiries, and assist with the sales process.

3. *<u>Sales Forecasting:</u>* Machine learning algorithms can forecast sales trends and optimize inventory management.

1.4 Social Selling

Social media platforms have become integral to the sales process:

1. *<u>Engagement</u>*: Sales professionals can engage with prospects and customers on platforms like LinkedIn, Twitter, and Facebook.

2. _**Lead Generation**_: Social media is a powerful tool for lead generation and building relationships.

3. _**Brand Building**_: Businesses can use social media to enhance their brand presence and reputation.

1.5 Customer-Centricity

The digital transformation has shifted the focus to customer-centric sales:

1. _**Personalization**_: Data and technology enable businesses to personalize their interactions with customers, delivering tailored experiences.

2. _**Customer Insights**_: Businesses can gather insights into customer preferences, behaviors, and feedback, driving continuous improvement.

3. _**Transparency**_: Digital platforms promote transparency in pricing, product information, and policies, fostering trust.

The digital transformation of sales has created a dynamic and competitive landscape. Embracing digital tools, data-driven insights, and customer-centricity is essential for sales professionals to thrive in this new era. As we continue our exploration of modern selling techniques, you'll discover how to harness the power of digital technology to connect with the modern buyer effectively. Welcome to the digital future of sales!

<u>Chapter 2: Building a Personal Brand for Sales</u>

- The Importance of Personal Branding
- Leveraging Social Media and Online Presence
- Becoming a Thought Leader in Your Industry

<u>Building a Personal Brand for Sales</u>

In the modern selling landscape, sales professionals are no longer just representatives of their companies; they are brands themselves. Building a personal brand is a powerful strategy for establishing trust, credibility, and influence in the digital age. In this chapter, we will explore the importance of personal branding in sales, provide insights into leveraging social media and online presence, and guide you on the path to becoming a thought leader in your industry.

The Importance of Personal Branding

In the digital age, personal branding has emerged as a powerful tool for professionals in various fields, including sales. Personal branding refers to the practice of creating and promoting a unique and authentic image of oneself to the world. For sales professionals, building a personal brand is not just an option; it's a strategic necessity. Here's why personal branding is of utmost importance:

1. Credibility and Trust

In the world of sales, trust is paramount. Buyers are more likely to do business with individuals they trust. Personal branding allows you to establish and enhance your credibility as a sales professional. When you have a well-defined personal brand that communicates your expertise and values, potential clients are more likely to trust you with their business.

2. Differentiation

The sales landscape is often crowded and competitive. Personal branding sets you apart from the competition. It's about showcasing what makes you unique, your approach to problem-solving, and your commitment to delivering value to clients. A strong personal brand ensures that you are not just seen as another salesperson but as someone with a distinct identity and value proposition.

3. Building Relationships

Sales is not just about transactions; it's about building lasting relationships. Personal branding fosters genuine connections with clients. When you authentically communicate your values and mission, you attract like-minded individuals and businesses. These connections can lead to long-term partnerships and repeat business.

4. Online Presence

In today's digital world, your online presence is often the first point of contact between you and potential clients. A well-crafted personal brand translates into a strong online presence. Your LinkedIn profile, social media accounts, and personal website are digital extensions of your personal brand. When prospects research you online, they should find a consistent and compelling narrative that reinforces your expertise and trustworthiness.

5. Career Advancement

Personal branding extends beyond your current role or company. It can significantly impact your career trajectory. A strong personal brand can attract new career opportunities, partnerships, and speaking engagements. It positions you as an authority in your field, making you a sought-after professional.

6. Adaptability

A well-established personal brand gives you a degree of flexibility and adaptability in your career. Whether you're changing industries, starting your own business, or exploring new roles, your personal brand remains a valuable asset. It follows you wherever your career journey takes you.

7. Influence and Thought Leadership

In sales, influence matters. A strong personal brand can transform you into a thought leader in your industry. When you consistently share valuable insights, engage in meaningful conversations, and contribute to industry discussions, you become a go-to expert. Your opinions carry weight, and your recommendations are trusted.

In conclusion, personal branding is not a superficial endeavor; it's a strategic imperative for sales professionals in the digital age. It's about showcasing your expertise, values, and personality authentically. Your personal brand becomes your unique selling proposition, helping you establish credibility, build trust, and excel in the competitive world of sales. In the following sections, we will delve into practical strategies for leveraging social media, online presence, and thought leadership to strengthen your personal brand in sales.

Leveraging Social Media and Online Presence

In the digital age, an online presence is the gateway to connecting with potential clients and building your personal brand as a sales professional. Social media platforms and your personal website are powerful tools that can help you reach a wider audience, showcase your expertise, and engage with your target market effectively. In this section, we will explore strategies for leveraging social media and optimizing your online presence to bolster your personal brand in sales.

3.1 The Digital Storefront: Your Online Presence

Your online presence serves as your digital storefront, making a significant first impression on potential clients. Here's how to make the most of it:

1. *Professional Website:* Consider creating a professional website that features your expertise, achievements, and portfolio. This serves as a centralized hub for showcasing your personal brand.

2. *LinkedIn Profile*: LinkedIn is a crucial platform for sales professionals. Ensure your LinkedIn profile is complete, professional, and highlights your achievements. Use a high-quality profile picture.

3. *Social Media Profiles*: Your social media profiles, including Twitter, Facebook, and Instagram, should align with your

personal brand. Use consistent branding elements such as profile pictures and cover images.

3.2 Content Sharing and Engagement

Content is the heart of your online presence. Sharing valuable content and engaging with your audience are key strategies for strengthening your personal brand:

1. ***Content Creation:*** Create and share content that demonstrates your expertise. This can include articles, blog posts, videos, infographics, and podcasts. Consistency is key.

2. ***Content Curation***: Curate and share relevant industry news and insights. This positions you as a knowledgeable resource in your field.

3. ***Engagement***: Actively engage with your network by commenting on posts, sharing

valuable insights, and participating in discussions. Engaging with others' content can also expand your reach.

3.3 Building Thought Leadership

Becoming a thought leader in your industry is a powerful way to boost your personal brand:

1. *Content Authority*: Share your expertise by creating in-depth, informative content. Write articles or whitepapers that provide valuable insights.

2. *Speaking Engagements:* Consider speaking at industry events, webinars, or conferences. These opportunities enhance your reputation as a thought leader.

3. *Networking with Influencers:* Connect with industry influencers and thought leaders. Collaborate on projects or engage in joint ventures to increase your visibility.

3.4 Authenticity and Consistency

Authenticity is the cornerstone of personal branding:

1. ***Be Yourself***: Authenticity is about being genuine and true to your values. Don't try to be someone you're not.

2. ***Consistency***: Maintain a consistent online presence. Regularly update your profiles, share content, and engage with your audience. Consistency reinforces your personal brand.

3.5 Analytics and Improvement

Use analytics tools to track the performance of your online presence:

1. ***Website Analytics:*** Monitor website traffic, engagement, and the performance of specific content.

2. ***Social Media Analytics***: Analyze engagement metrics such as likes, shares, and comments. Identify which content resonates most with your audience.

3. ***Adjust and Optimize***: Use data-driven insights to refine your content strategy and engagement tactics. Continuously improve your online presence.

Your online presence is a dynamic and evolving asset that can significantly impact your personal brand as a sales professional. By leveraging social media, sharing valuable content, and consistently engaging with your audience, you'll strengthen your digital footprint and position yourself as a trusted authority in your field. In the following chapters, we will explore additional strategies for becoming a successful sales professional in the digital age.

Becoming a Thought Leader in Your Industry

Becoming a thought leader in your industry is a powerful way to elevate your personal brand and establish yourself as an authority. Thought leaders are respected experts whose opinions and insights are highly valued by their peers, clients, and the broader community. In this section, we will delve into the strategies and actions you can take to become a thought leader in your industry within the realm of sales.

4.1 Content Authority

Content creation is at the heart of thought leadership. Here's how to establish yourself as a content authority:

1. *In-Depth Content*: Create in-depth, informative content that addresses complex topics or challenges within your industry. This can include articles, blog posts, research papers, or e-books.

2. *__Original Research__*: Conduct original research or surveys related to your industry. Share the findings and insights through reports or articles.

3. *__Case Studies__*: Share real-world case studies that showcase your expertise in solving specific industry-related problems.

4. *__Consistent Publishing__*: Maintain a consistent publishing schedule. Regularly share valuable content to keep your audience engaged.

4.2 Speaking Engagements

Speaking at industry events, webinars, conferences, or podcasts can significantly enhance your thought leadership:

1. *__Submit Proposals__*: Propose speaking topics or presentations to relevant industry events and conferences.

2. *__Webinars and Podcasts__*: Host or participate in webinars and podcasts to share your insights and expertise with a broader audience.

3. *__Workshops and Training__*: Offer workshops or training sessions within your industry niche.

4.3 Networking with Influencers

Building relationships with industry influencers and thought leaders can boost your own reputation:

1. *__Connect and Engage__*: Reach out to influencers in your industry through social media or email. Engage with their content and provide thoughtful comments.

2. *__Collaborations__*: Collaborate on projects, webinars, or articles with influencers. Joint ventures can expand your reach.

3. *__Interviews and Guest Posts__*: Offer to interview influencers for your own content or contribute guest posts to their platforms.

4.4 Publish a Book or Whitepaper

Authoring a book or whitepaper on a relevant industry topic can solidify your thought leadership:

1. *__Book Writing__*: Consider writing a book that shares your expertise and insights. Self-publishing is an option, or you can seek traditional publishing routes.

2. *__Whitepapers__*: Produce whitepapers that delve into industry trends, challenges, or solutions.

4.5 Active Industry Involvement

Active participation in industry organizations and associations can enhance your thought leadership:

1. *__Join Associations__*: Become a member of relevant industry associations or organizations. Attend conferences and participate in committees.

2. *__Leadership Roles__*: Seek leadership roles within these organizations, such as serving on boards or committees.

4.6 Consistent Personal Branding

Ensure your personal brand aligns with your thought leadership goals:

1. *__Content Cohesion__*: Ensure that your personal branding across all platforms and content is consistent and aligned with your expertise.

2. ***Online Presence***: Maintain a strong and professional online presence, including a polished LinkedIn profile and a personal website.

3. ***Thought Leadership Positioning***: Clearly position yourself as a thought leader in your industry, both in your branding and content.

Becoming a thought leader is a journey that requires dedication, expertise, and a commitment to sharing valuable insights. Over time, your thought leadership will enhance your personal brand, attract a loyal following, and open doors to exciting opportunities within your industry. As you continue to cultivate your thought leadership, you'll find your influence and impact in the industry growing steadily.

Chapter 3: Data-Driven Selling

- The Power of Data in Sales
- Utilizing CRM Systems
- Predictive Analytics for Sales

In today's hyper-connected world, data has become an invaluable asset for sales professionals. Data-driven selling is the practice of leveraging data to inform and enhance every aspect of the sales process. From understanding customer behavior to predicting future trends, data-driven selling empowers sales teams to make informed decisions, streamline operations, and, ultimately, drive revenue growth. This chapter delves into the power of data in sales, the utilization of Customer Relationship Management (CRM) systems, and the application of predictive analytics for sales success.

3.1 The Power of Data in Sales

Data is the foundation upon which effective sales strategies are built. Here's how data empowers sales professionals:

1. *Customer Insights*: Data provides invaluable insights into customer behavior, preferences, and buying patterns. By analyzing this data, sales teams can tailor their approach to individual customers and create more personalized interactions.

2. *Lead Prioritization*: Not all leads are created equal. Data-driven tools can help sales teams prioritize leads based on factors such as likelihood to convert and potential value, ensuring that resources are allocated where they are most likely to yield results.

3. *Sales Performance Metrics*: Data allows sales managers to track the performance of their teams, identifying areas of strength and improvement. Metrics such

as conversion rates, sales cycle length, and customer acquisition cost provide actionable insights.

4. ***Competitor Analysis***: Data-driven competitive analysis helps sales professionals understand the strengths and weaknesses of competitors, enabling them to position their offerings more effectively.

5. ***Sales Forecasting***: Predictive analytics can help sales teams forecast future sales trends with greater accuracy, allowing for better resource allocation and strategic planning.

3.2 Utilizing CRM Systems

Customer Relationship Management (CRM) systems are essential tools for data-driven selling. These platforms enable sales professionals to centralize customer data, streamline communication, and enhance customer relationships. Here's how CRM systems contribute to sales success:

1. ***Data Centralization***: CRM systems consolidate customer data, including contact information, purchase history, and communication history. This centralization ensures that all team members have access to the most up-to-date information.

2. ***Efficient Communication***: CRM systems facilitate communication by providing a unified platform for emails, calls, and messaging. This ensures that sales teams can respond to customer inquiries promptly.

3. ***Lead Tracking***: CRM systems track leads through the sales pipeline, allowing sales professionals to monitor progress and identify potential bottlenecks.

4. _Automation_: Many CRM systems offer automation features, such as automated email responses and lead nurturing workflows. These automation tools save time and ensure consistent communication.

5. _Reporting and Analytics_: CRM systems provide robust reporting and analytics capabilities. Sales managers can generate reports on key metrics, helping them make data-driven decisions.

3.3 Predictive Analytics for Sales

Predictive analytics is a powerful tool in data-driven selling, allowing sales teams to anticipate customer behavior and trends. Here's how predictive analytics can be applied to sales:

1. _Lead Scoring_: Predictive analytics assigns scores to leads based on their likelihood to convert. Sales teams can focus their

efforts on high-scoring leads, increasing efficiency.

2. _**Sales Forecasting**_: Predictive models analyze historical sales data and market trends to forecast future sales. This enables sales managers to make informed decisions about resource allocation and goal setting.

3. _**Customer Churn Prediction**_: Predictive analytics can identify customers who are at risk of churning (leaving). Sales teams can proactively address their concerns and retain valuable clients.

4. _**Cross-Selling and Upselling**_: Predictive models can suggest additional products or services that existing customers are likely to be interested in, increasing revenue opportunities.

5. _**Inventory Management**_: Predictive analytics can optimize inventory

management by forecasting demand, reducing overstock, and minimizing stockouts.

In conclusion, data-driven selling is not just a trend; it's a fundamental shift in how sales professionals approach their roles. The power of data, harnessed through CRM systems and predictive analytics, enables sales teams to operate with greater efficiency, make informed decisions, and provide a more personalized customer experience. As you delve deeper into data-driven selling, you'll uncover additional techniques and tools that can transform your sales strategies and drive success in the modern business landscape.

Chapter 4: Inbound Marketing and Lead Generation

- Attracting, Engaging, and Delighting Customers
- Content Marketing Strategies
- SEO and Its Impact on Sales

Inbound marketing has revolutionized the way businesses approach customer acquisition and lead generation. It is a customer-centric approach that focuses on attracting, engaging, and delighting customers through valuable content and meaningful interactions. In this chapter, we will explore the core concepts of inbound marketing and lead generation, including strategies for attracting prospects, the role of content marketing, and the importance of Search Engine Optimization (SEO) in driving sales.

4.1 Attracting, Engaging, and Delighting Customers

Inbound marketing operates on the principle of attracting, engaging, and delighting customers at every stage of their journey. Here's how each of these components plays a crucial role in the lead generation process:

1. *Attract*: Attracting potential customers begins with understanding their needs and pain points. By creating content and resources that address these issues, businesses can draw prospects to their website and online platforms. This content can take the form of blog posts, videos, ebooks, webinars, and more.

2. *Engage*: Once prospects are attracted, engagement becomes the focus. Engagement involves nurturing relationships with prospects by providing them with relevant and valuable information. This can be achieved through

personalized email campaigns, social media interactions, and educational content that guides prospects through their decision-making process.

3. *Delight*: Delighting customers is about exceeding their expectations after the sale. Happy customers become promoters of your brand, leading to referrals and repeat business. Delight can be achieved through exceptional customer service, ongoing support, and providing valuable resources and insights even after the purchase.

4.2 Content Marketing Strategies

Content marketing is at the core of inbound marketing and lead generation. Here are key strategies for implementing effective content marketing:

1. *Understanding Your Audience*: To create content that resonates with your target audience, it's essential to understand their

preferences, pain points, and needs. Conducting market research and creating buyer personas can help in this regard.

2. *Quality Over Quantity*: While consistency is important, the quality of your content should never be compromised. High-quality, informative, and engaging content will attract and retain more prospects.

3. *Diverse Content Types*: Experiment with various content types to cater to different learning styles and preferences. This can include blog posts, videos, infographics, podcasts, and more.

4. *Content Calendar*: Create a content calendar to plan and schedule your content in advance. A well-structured calendar ensures a steady flow of content and helps maintain consistency.

5. _**SEO Optimization**_: Incorporate SEO best practices to make your content more discoverable. This includes keyword research, on-page SEO, and optimizing meta descriptions and titles.

4.3 SEO and Its Impact on Sales

Search Engine Optimization (SEO) is a critical element of inbound marketing and lead generation. It involves optimizing your online content to rank higher in search engine results pages (SERPs). Here's why SEO is vital for driving sales:

1. _**Increased Visibility**_: By optimizing your content for relevant keywords, you increase the chances of your website and content being found by potential customers when they search for information related to your industry or products.

2. _**Credibility and Trust**_: Websites that rank higher in search results are often perceived as more credible and trustworthy by users. This credibility can positively impact a prospect's decision to engage with your business.

3. _**Targeted Traffic**_: SEO helps attract highly targeted traffic to your website. When your content aligns with the search intent of users, you're more likely to attract prospects who are genuinely interested in your products or services.

4. _**Competitive Advantage**_: Businesses that invest in SEO gain a competitive advantage. If your competitors are not optimizing their online presence for search, you can capture a larger share of the market.

5. _**Long-Term Results**_: Unlike some other forms of marketing, SEO can deliver long-term results. Once your content ranks

well, it continues to attract organic traffic over time without the ongoing costs associated with paid advertising.

In conclusion, inbound marketing and lead generation have transformed how businesses connect with and acquire customers. By focusing on attracting, engaging, and delighting prospects through valuable content and optimizing that content for search engines, businesses can drive sales and build lasting customer relationships. As you delve deeper into these strategies, you'll discover the nuances of inbound marketing that can propel your lead generation efforts to new heights.

Chapter 5: The Art of Sales Prospecting

- Effective Prospecting Techniques
- Identifying Ideal Customers
- Sales Automation Tools for Prospecting

Sales prospecting is the lifeblood of any successful sales operation. It's the process of identifying and reaching out to potential customers who have a genuine need for your product or service. In this chapter, we'll explore the art of sales prospecting, including effective techniques, strategies for identifying ideal customers, and the role of sales automation tools in streamlining the prospecting process.

5.1 Effective Prospecting Techniques

Successful sales prospecting requires a combination of strategies and techniques to identify and engage with potential customers. Here are some effective prospecting techniques:

1. _Cold Calling_: While traditional, cold calling remains a viable method for prospecting. Prepare a compelling script and focus on building a rapport with the prospect.

2. _Email Outreach_: Craft personalized and concise email messages to introduce yourself and your offering. Avoid generic, spammy emails, and instead, provide value from the very first interaction.

3. _Social Selling_: Leverage social media platforms like LinkedIn, Twitter, and Facebook to connect with potential customers. Share valuable content, engage in meaningful conversations, and establish yourself as a knowledgeable resource.

4. _Networking_: Attend industry events, conferences, and networking meetups to expand your contacts. Building relationships in person can be highly effective for prospecting.

5. *Referrals*: Existing customers or contacts can be excellent sources of referrals. Ask for referrals from satisfied clients, and offer incentives if appropriate.

6. *Content Marketing*: Create informative and educational content that addresses common pain points or challenges faced by your target audience. Content marketing can attract prospects to your website or social profiles.

7. *Partnerships*: Collaborate with complementary businesses or industry partners to access their customer base. Partnerships can open up new prospecting avenues.

5.2 Identifying Ideal Customers

Prospecting becomes more efficient and fruitful when you focus on identifying and targeting ideal customers. Here's how to do it:

1. *<u>Create Buyer Personas</u>*: Develop detailed buyer personas that represent your ideal customers. Consider factors like demographics, job roles, challenges, and goals.

2. *<u>Segment Your Audience</u>*: Divide your prospecting efforts into segments based on criteria like industry, company size, or geographical location. Tailor your approach to each segment.

3. *<u>Analyze Data</u>*: Use data and analytics to identify patterns in your existing customer base. This can help pinpoint common traits and characteristics of your ideal customers.

4. *<u>Qualify Leads</u>*: Implement lead scoring to prioritize prospects based on their likelihood to convert. Not all leads are equally valuable; focus on those that align with your ideal customer profile.

5.3 Sales Automation Tools for Prospecting

Sales automation tools can significantly streamline the prospecting process and improve efficiency:

1. ***Customer Relationship Management (CRM) Systems***: CRMs centralize customer data, track interactions, and automate follow-ups. They help sales professionals manage leads and customers more effectively.

2. ***Email Marketing Platforms***: Email marketing tools enable you to send automated, personalized email campaigns to prospects at various stages of the sales funnel.

3. ***Sales Engagement Platforms***: These platforms provide a suite of tools for outreach, follow-ups, and tracking. They often integrate with CRMs to provide a comprehensive prospecting solution.

4. *__Lead Generation Software__*: Tools like lead generation software can identify potential leads based on criteria you specify, saving you time on manual research.

5. *__Social Media Management Tools__*: These tools allow you to schedule and automate social media posts and engagement, ensuring a consistent online presence.

6. *__Sales Intelligence Platforms__*: These platforms provide valuable insights about prospects, including contact information, company details, and social media profiles.

In conclusion, sales prospecting is an art that requires a strategic approach, an understanding of your ideal customers, and the right tools to streamline the process. By implementing effective prospecting techniques, focusing on your ideal customer profile, and leveraging sales automation tools, you can build a robust pipeline of potential customers and increase your chances of closing deals. In the following chapters, we will continue to explore advanced strategies for success in the world of modern sales.

Chapter 6: Building Strong Customer Relationships

- Nurturing Leads into Loyal Customers
- Effective Communication in Modern Sales
- Customer Relationship Management (CRM)

In the world of modern sales, building strong customer relationships is not just a priority; it's a necessity. In this chapter, we will explore the strategies and techniques essential for nurturing leads into loyal customers, the importance of effective communication in the context of contemporary sales, and the role of Customer Relationship Management (CRM) systems in managing and enhancing customer relationships.

6.1 Nurturing Leads into Loyal Customers

The process of turning leads into loyal customers is a delicate and ongoing journey that requires a combination of understanding, engagement, and trust-building:

1. _**Lead Nurturing**_: Not every lead is ready to make a purchase immediately. Lead nurturing involves guiding prospects through the decision-making process by providing them with relevant information, addressing their concerns, and staying top-of-mind until they are ready to buy.

2. _**Personalization**_: Personalization is key to building rapport and trust. Address prospects by their name, tailor your communication to their interests and pain points, and provide solutions that genuinely meet their needs.

3. _**Timely Follow-Up**_: Prompt and attentive follow-up is crucial. When a prospect expresses interest or reaches out with questions, responding quickly demonstrates your commitment and professionalism.

4. *__Educational Content__*: Continue to provide valuable content that educates prospects about your products or services. This content can take the form of blog posts, webinars, whitepapers, or how-to guides.

5. *__Feedback Loop__*: Encourage feedback from leads and customers. This not only shows that you value their input but also provides insights into areas where you can improve your products or services.

6.2 Effective Communication in Modern Sales

Effective communication is the cornerstone of successful customer relationships in the modern sales landscape. Here are key elements of effective communication:

1. *__Active Listening__*: Truly understanding a prospect's needs requires active listening. Pay attention to their words, ask clarifying questions, and show empathy.

2. ***Multichannel Communication***: Modern sales involve communication across various channels, including email, phone, social media, and messaging apps. Adapt your communication to the preferred channel of your prospect.

3. ***Transparent and Honest Communication***: Honesty and transparency build trust. Be clear about what you can offer, and don't make promises you can't keep.

4. ***Value-Oriented Messaging***: Every communication should provide value. Whether it's sharing industry insights, addressing a pain point, or offering a solution, ensure that your interactions contribute positively to the prospect's experience.

5. ***Timely Follow-Up***: Timeliness is critical. Whether it's responding to inquiries,

sending requested information, or following up after a sale, being prompt shows respect for the prospect's time.

6.3 Customer Relationship Management (CRM)

CRM systems are indispensable tools for managing and enhancing customer relationships. Here's how CRM can empower modern sales:

1. ***Data Centralization***: CRM systems centralize customer data, providing a comprehensive view of each customer's history, interactions, and preferences.

2. ***Automation***: CRM automates routine tasks such as lead tracking, email follow-ups, and appointment scheduling. Automation ensures that leads and customers receive timely and personalized communication.

3. ***Lead Scoring:*** CRM systems often include lead scoring capabilities, which help prioritize leads based on their readiness to buy. This ensures that sales efforts are focused on prospects with the highest potential.

4. ***Analytics and Reporting***: CRM systems provide robust analytics and reporting features, allowing sales teams to track performance, measure the effectiveness of campaigns, and make data-driven decisions.

5. ***Customer Segmentation***: CRM enables customer segmentation, allowing sales teams to tailor their communication and marketing efforts to different segments based on demographics, behavior, or interests.

In conclusion, building strong customer relationships is not only about closing deals but also about fostering trust, providing value, and creating loyal advocates for your brand. By nurturing leads into loyal customers through personalized communication, transparency, and the strategic use of CRM systems, modern sales professionals can thrive in an environment where lasting customer relationships are the foundation of success. In the following chapters, we will explore additional strategies for sales excellence in the digital age.

Chapter 7: Sales Technology and Automation

- Leveraging Sales Technology
- Automation in Sales Outreach
- AI and Machine Learning in Sales

In the rapidly evolving landscape of modern sales, technology and automation have become pivotal tools for sales professionals. This chapter explores the role of sales technology, the benefits of automation in sales outreach, and the growing impact of artificial intelligence (AI) and machine learning on the sales process.

7.1 Leveraging Sales Technology

Sales technology encompasses a wide range of tools and platforms designed to enhance the efficiency and effectiveness of sales efforts. Here's how sales technology can empower sales professionals:

1. ***Customer Relationship Management (CRM) Systems:*** CRMs serve as central hubs for managing customer and prospect information. They track interactions, store contact details, and provide insights into customer behavior and preferences.

2. ***Sales Engagement Platforms***: These platforms streamline sales outreach by automating tasks like email sequencing, follow-ups, and appointment scheduling. They often integrate with CRMs to ensure a seamless workflow.

3. ***Predictive Analytics***: Predictive analytics tools use data to forecast sales trends, identify potential leads, and prioritize prospects with a higher likelihood to convert.

4. ***Communication Tools***: Video conferencing, chat, and messaging apps facilitate real-time communication with prospects and customers. They enable

virtual meetings, product demonstrations, and support.

5. ***Sales Enablement Platforms***: These platforms equip sales teams with the content and resources they need, such as sales collateral, training materials, and playbooks.

6. ***E-commerce and Online Sales Platforms***: E-commerce platforms enable businesses to sell products or services online, providing a convenient way for customers to make purchases.

7.2 Automation in Sales Outreach

Automation plays a crucial role in sales outreach, allowing sales professionals to engage with leads and prospects at scale while maintaining a personalized touch. Here are key aspects of automation in sales outreach:

1. *Email Sequencing*: Automation tools can schedule and send a series of personalized email messages to prospects. These sequences can nurture leads, follow up after initial contact, and provide valuable content.

2. *Lead Nurturing Workflows*: Workflow automation allows sales teams to automate lead nurturing processes. For example, when a lead downloads an ebook, an automated workflow can trigger a series of emails and follow-up tasks.

3. *Appointment Scheduling*: Tools like online scheduling apps enable prospects to book appointments at their convenience, eliminating the back-and-forth of scheduling.

4. *Social Media Automation*: Social media management tools can schedule posts, track engagement, and automate responses to messages and comments.

5. ***Chatbots and AI-Powered Assistants***: Chatbots and AI-driven virtual assistants can engage with website visitors, answer common questions, and qualify leads in real time.

7.3 AI and Machine Learning in Sales

The integration of AI and machine learning is reshaping the sales landscape. These technologies offer advanced capabilities that enhance sales processes:

1. ***Predictive Lead Scoring***: AI algorithms analyze historical data to predict which leads are most likely to convert. This enables sales teams to prioritize high-value prospects.

2. ***Sales Forecasting***: Machine learning models analyze sales data and market trends to provide more accurate sales forecasts, aiding in resource allocation and planning.

3. *Personalization*:   AI-driven
personalization tailors content and
recommendations to individual prospects,
increasing engagement and conversion
rates.

4. *Sales Analytics*: AI-powered analytics
tools provide deep insights into customer
behavior, helping sales teams refine their
strategies.

5. *Chatbots and Virtual Assistants:*
AI-driven chatbots and virtual assistants
can handle routine inquiries, freeing up
sales professionals to focus on high-value
tasks.

6. *Voice Recognition*:   Voice-activated
technology is increasingly used for sales
calls and virtual meetings, improving
convenience and productivity.

In conclusion, sales technology and automation
are transforming the sales profession. By

leveraging the right tools and platforms, sales professionals can streamline processes, engage with prospects more effectively, and ultimately drive revenue growth. Additionally, the integration of AI and machine learning promises to further enhance sales efficiency and customer insights. As you continue to explore these technologies and adapt to the changing sales landscape, you'll be better equipped to excel in the world of modern sales.

Chapter 8: Social Selling

- The Role of Social Media in Sales
- Strategies for Successful Social Selling
- Measuring Social Selling ROI

In the era of digital connectivity, social selling has emerged as a powerful approach for sales professionals to build relationships, engage with prospects, and ultimately drive sales. This chapter explores the role of social media in sales, strategies for successful social selling, and methods for measuring the return on investment (ROI) of your social selling efforts.

8.1 The Role of Social Media in Sales

Social media has transformed the way businesses connect with their audiences, and it's now an integral part of the sales process. Here's how social media plays a pivotal role in sales:

1. *Expanded Reach*: Social media platforms offer access to a vast and diverse

audience. Sales professionals can connect with prospects, customers, industry influencers, and decision-makers from around the world.

2. **_Building Relationships_**: Social media provides a platform for building and nurturing relationships with leads and prospects. It allows for ongoing interactions and personalized communication.

3. **_Brand Visibility_**: An active social media presence enhances brand visibility and credibility. When prospects see your brand engaging thoughtfully and consistently, it instills trust.

4. **_Content Sharing_**: Sales professionals can share valuable content such as blog posts, videos, infographics, and industry insights to educate and engage their audience. This positions them as experts in their field.

5. _**Listening and Research**_: Social media enables sales professionals to listen to conversations and gather insights about their target audience. This information can inform their sales strategies.

8.2 Strategies for Successful Social Selling

Effective social selling involves more than just having a social media profile. It requires a strategic approach to engage with prospects and guide them through the sales journey. Here are some strategies for successful social selling:

1. _**Optimize Your Profiles**_: Ensure your social media profiles are complete and professional. Use a clear profile picture, write a compelling bio, and provide contact information.

2. _**Identify Your Target Audience**_: Determine your ideal customers and where they spend their time on social

media. Focus your efforts on platforms that align with your audience.

3. _**Content Sharing**_: Share valuable, relevant content that addresses your audience's pain points and interests. Create a content calendar to maintain consistency.

4. _**Engage Authentically**_: Engage with your audience by responding to comments, messages, and mentions. Show genuine interest in their needs and questions.

5. _**Use Social Listening**_: Monitor social media for mentions of your brand, competitors, and industry trends. This information can inform your sales conversations.

6. _**Build Relationships**_: Focus on building meaningful relationships rather than immediately pushing for a sale. Offer help, provide solutions, and establish trust.

7. _**Leverage LinkedIn**_: LinkedIn is a powerhouse for B2B social selling. Connect with relevant professionals, join industry groups, and use InMail for personalized outreach.

8. _**Social Selling Tools**_: Utilize social selling tools and platforms that offer features like lead tracking, social listening, and analytics.

8.3 Measuring Social Selling ROI

To determine the impact of your social selling efforts, you need to measure ROI. Here's how you can measure the return on investment of your social selling activities:

1. _**Engagement Metrics**_: Track engagement metrics such as likes, shares, comments, and follows on your social media posts. These metrics indicate the level of interest and interaction your content generates.

2. *__Lead Generation__*: Measure the number of leads generated through social media efforts. Use tracking links and landing pages to attribute leads to specific social posts or campaigns.

3. *__Conversion Rate__*: Calculate the conversion rate of social media leads into paying customers. This helps determine the effectiveness of your social selling strategies.

4. *__Revenue Attribution__*: Analyze how much revenue can be directly attributed to your social selling efforts. This may involve tracking sales generated from social media referrals or campaigns.

5. *__Customer Lifetime Value (CLV)__*: Consider the long-term impact of social selling by calculating the CLV of customers acquired through social media channels.

6. *<u>Costs vs. Returns</u>*: Compare the costs of your social selling activities (e.g., advertising spend, social media management tools) to the returns generated in terms of leads and revenue.

7. *<u>Customer Feedback</u>*: Collect feedback from customers who engaged with your brand through social media. Their insights can provide qualitative data on the impact of your efforts.

In conclusion, social selling is a dynamic and influential approach in modern sales. By harnessing the power of social media, sales professionals can expand their reach, build relationships, and drive sales. Implementing effective social selling strategies and measuring ROI are essential steps in maximizing the benefits of this approach. As you refine your social selling skills, you'll be better positioned to thrive in the ever-evolving world of digital sales.

Chapter 9: Virtual Selling in the Digital Age

- The Rise of Virtual Sales Meetings
- Virtual Selling Best Practices
- Overcoming Virtual Selling Challenges

In today's digital age, virtual selling has become a cornerstone of modern sales. This chapter delves into the rise of virtual sales meetings, best practices for successful virtual selling, and strategies for overcoming the unique challenges presented by virtual selling.

9.1 The Rise of Virtual Sales Meetings

The shift to virtual sales meetings has been accelerated by advancements in technology, changing consumer behavior, and the global shift towards remote work. Here's why virtual sales meetings have risen to prominence:

1. *Global Reach*: Virtual meetings break down geographical barriers, enabling sales

professionals to connect with prospects and clients worldwide without the need for travel.

2. *Cost-Efficiency*: Virtual sales meetings reduce travel expenses, making it a more cost-effective approach for businesses. This cost savings can be allocated to other sales and marketing efforts.

3. *Time Savings*: Virtual meetings save time for both sales professionals and clients. Meetings can be scheduled more conveniently, reducing downtime and increasing productivity.

4. *Flexibility*: Sales professionals can conduct virtual meetings from anywhere with an internet connection. This flexibility allows for greater adaptability in meeting the needs of clients.

5. *Technology Integration*: Advances in virtual meeting technology, including

video conferencing, screen sharing, and interactive presentations, enhance the virtual selling experience.

9.2 Virtual Selling Best Practices

Successful virtual selling requires a strategic approach that maximizes the impact of digital interactions. Here are some best practices for effective virtual selling:

1. *Preparation*: Prepare for virtual meetings just as you would for in-person meetings. Familiarize yourself with the technology, review the agenda, and understand the client's needs.

2. *Engaging Presentation*: Keep virtual meetings engaging with interactive presentations, visuals, and multimedia content. Avoid overly lengthy monologues.

3. *__Video Etiquette__*: When using video conferencing, maintain professional etiquette. Dress appropriately, ensure proper lighting, and maintain eye contact with the camera.

4. *__Clear Communication__*: Ensure clear and concise communication. Speak slowly, enunciate, and actively listen to clients to avoid misunderstandings.

5. *__Customization__*: Tailor your virtual selling approach to each client's preferences. Some clients may prefer video calls, while others may prefer phone calls or email communication.

6. *__Follow-Up__*: Promptly follow up after virtual meetings with personalized summaries and action items. This reinforces your commitment to the client's needs.

7. _Security_: Be mindful of data security and privacy during virtual meetings. Use secure communication platforms and protect sensitive information.

8. _**Technical Support**_: Have technical support available during meetings in case of technical issues or challenges.

9.3 Overcoming Virtual Selling Challenges

While virtual selling offers numerous benefits, it also presents unique challenges that sales professionals must navigate effectively:

1. _**Lack of Personal Connection**_: Building rapport and trust can be more challenging in virtual settings. Overcome this by showing empathy, active listening, and authentic engagement.

2. _**Technology Issues:**_ Technical glitches and connectivity problems can disrupt virtual meetings. Have backup plans in place and

be prepared to address these issues professionally.

3. *Distractions*: Both you and your clients may face distractions during virtual meetings. Minimize distractions on your end and politely address any distractions on the client's end.

4. *Loss of Non-Verbal Cues*: In virtual meetings, non-verbal cues like body language may be less visible. Pay attention to vocal cues and verbal signals to understand the client's reactions.

5. *Security Concerns*: Protecting sensitive information and ensuring data security are critical. Use secure platforms, encrypt communication, and educate clients about security measures.

6. *Screen Fatigue*: Prolonged virtual meetings can lead to screen fatigue. Schedule shorter, more focused meetings and allow for breaks when necessary.

In conclusion, virtual selling has become a fundamental aspect of modern sales, offering convenience, efficiency, and global reach. By adhering to best practices and addressing the unique challenges of virtual selling, sales professionals can continue to build strong client relationships, meet client needs effectively, and drive sales success in the digital age. As virtual selling continues to evolve, embracing these strategies will be crucial for staying ahead in the competitive sales landscape.

Chapter 10: The Future of Modern Selling

- Emerging Trends and Technologies
- Preparing for the Sales Landscape of Tomorrow
- Continuous Learning and Adaptation

The future of modern selling is an ever-evolving landscape influenced by emerging trends, disruptive technologies, and changing customer behaviors. In this chapter, we explore the exciting possibilities of the sales landscape of tomorrow, strategies for preparing for these changes, and the importance of continuous learning and adaptation.

10.1 Emerging Trends and Technologies

As we look ahead to the future of modern selling, several trends and technologies are poised to shape the sales profession:

1. ***<u>Artificial Intelligence (AI) and Machine Learning</u>***: AI-driven insights and automation will continue to enhance sales processes, from predictive lead scoring to personalized recommendations and chatbot interactions.

2. ***<u>Augmented Reality (AR) and Virtual Reality (VR):</u>*** These technologies will revolutionize product demonstrations and customer experiences, allowing prospects to interact with products virtually.

3. ***<u>Blockchain</u>***: Blockchain technology offers transparency and security in transactions, which can be particularly valuable in complex B2B sales.

4. ***<u>Data Analytics</u>***: Advanced analytics tools will provide deeper customer insights, enabling more precise targeting and personalized sales strategies.

5. _**Remote Work**_: Remote work is here to stay, influencing how sales teams collaborate and connect with clients. Virtual selling and remote relationship-building will become even more critical.

6. _**Sustainability and Ethics:**_ Ethical and sustainable business practices will be central to sales, as conscious consumers prioritize companies with a positive social and environmental impact.

7. _**Personalization**_: Hyper-personalization, driven by AI, will enable sales professionals to create highly tailored experiences for each prospect.

8. _**Voice and Conversational AI**_: Voice-activated technology and conversational AI will become integral to sales interactions, from virtual assistants to voice-activated sales calls.

<u>**10.2 Preparing for the Sales Landscape of Tomorrow**</u>

To thrive in the evolving sales landscape of the future, sales professionals and organizations should consider the following strategies:

1. <u>***Embrace Technology:***</u> Stay informed about emerging technologies and their applications in sales. Embrace tools and platforms that enhance efficiency and effectiveness.

2. <u>***Agile Mindset***</u>: Develop an agile mindset that welcomes change and adaptation. The ability to pivot and innovate will be essential in a dynamic sales environment.

3. <u>***Customer-Centric Approach***</u>: Maintain a customer-centric approach, prioritizing the needs and preferences of clients. Building authentic relationships will remain a cornerstone of success.

4. ***Cross-Functional   Collaboration***:
Collaborate across departments, including marketing, customer support, and product development, to ensure a holistic customer experience.

5. ***Ethical Selling:*** Prioritize ethical selling practices that align with customer values and demonstrate a commitment to responsible business.

6. ***Continuous Learning***: Invest in ongoing education and professional development to stay up-to-date with industry trends and sharpen your skills.

7. ***Adaptation***: Be prepared to adapt to changing customer behaviors and preferences. Monitor customer feedback and market shifts closely.

10.3 Continuous Learning and Adaptation

In the rapidly evolving world of modern selling, continuous learning and adaptation are not optional; they are imperative. Here's why these practices are vital:

1. ***Staying Relevant:*** Continuous learning keeps you informed about the latest trends, technologies, and best practices, ensuring that you remain relevant in the field.

2. ***Enhancing Skills***: Ongoing education allows you to enhance your skills, whether it's mastering new sales techniques, improving communication, or becoming proficient with emerging tools.

3. ***Adaptability***: Adapting to change is a hallmark of successful sales professionals. Continuous learning equips you to pivot and thrive in an ever-changing landscape.

4. ***Competitive Edge:*** In a competitive market, staying ahead of the curve can

give you a significant competitive edge, enabling you to provide better value to your clients.

5. ***Professional Growth:*** Continuous learning is a journey of professional growth and personal development. It keeps you engaged, motivated, and passionate about your sales career.

As we look to the future of modern selling, embracing emerging trends and technologies, preparing for change, and committing to continuous learning and adaptation will be essential for sales professionals and organizations alike. The sales landscape of tomorrow offers exciting opportunities for those who are proactive and forward-thinking, ready to meet the evolving needs of customers in a digital and interconnected world.

<u>Conclusion</u>

The journey through the world of modern selling has been nothing short of transformative. We've explored the evolution of sales from traditional approaches to the dynamic digital landscape of today. We've delved into the power of technology, the rise of virtual selling, and the strategies for success in an ever-evolving field. As we conclude our exploration, let's reflect on the key takeaways and the path ahead for modern sales professionals.

<u>A Dynamic Evolution</u>:

Sales has come a long way, evolving with the times and adapting to the changing needs and preferences of customers. Traditional sales methods, while not obsolete, have been complemented by a host of technological advancements that have reshaped the way we connect, engage, and transact with clients.

<u>The Role of Technology</u>:

Technology has emerged as an indispensable ally in the modern sales journey. Customer Relationship Management (CRM) systems, automation tools, artificial intelligence, and data analytics have empowered sales professionals to streamline processes, personalize interactions, and make data-driven decisions. These tools have paved the way for efficiency and effectiveness in the sales profession.

The Power of Virtual Selling:

Virtual selling has revolutionized the sales landscape, offering global reach, cost efficiency, and flexibility. With the rise of remote work and digital connectivity, virtual sales meetings have become the norm. Sales professionals have learned to adapt, using video conferencing, interactive presentations, and engaging content to bridge the gap between physical distances.

Strategies for Success:

Successful modern selling is not solely reliant on technology; it is equally rooted in the fundamentals of building relationships, understanding customer needs, and delivering value. Strategies like social selling, data-driven insights, and ethical practices have been key drivers of success.

Preparing for Tomorrow:

As we look ahead, the future of modern selling promises even more exciting possibilities. Emerging technologies like augmented reality, blockchain, and voice-activated AI are set to reshape the sales landscape once again. To thrive in this dynamic environment, sales professionals must embrace change, prioritize the customer experience, and commit to continuous learning and adaptation.

The Ongoing Journey:

The world of modern selling is a journey, not a destination. It requires dedication, innovation, and a deep commitment to understanding and serving the needs of clients. In this journey, you are not alone. You are part of a vibrant community of sales professionals, each contributing their unique skills and insights to this ever-evolving field.

As you move forward in your modern sales journey, remember that your success is not solely defined by the deals you close but by the relationships you build, the value you provide, and the positive impact you have on your clients and your industry. Continue to adapt, learn, and grow, and you will be well-prepared to navigate the exciting and dynamic future of modern selling.

Thank you for joining us on this exploration of modern selling. May your sales career be filled with growth, fulfillment, and the satisfaction of helping your clients succeed in an increasingly interconnected world. Here's to the future of modern selling and the endless possibilities it holds.

Acknowledgments

A creative endeavor, such as writing a book on creative entrepreneurship, is not a solitary pursuit. It involves the contributions, support, and inspiration of many individuals and resources. We would like to express our heartfelt gratitude to those who have played a significant role in bringing this book to fruition.

Our Thanks Go To:

- God Almighty

- Creative Minds: To all the creative entrepreneurs and artists who generously shared their experiences, insights, and stories. Your contributions have enriched the content of this book and inspired countless others on their entrepreneurial journeys.

- Mentors and Advisors: To the mentors and advisors who provided guidance, expertise, and valuable feedback throughout the writing process. Your wisdom and experience have been invaluable.

- Readers and Supporters: To the readers and supporters who have shown interest in this book from its inception. Your enthusiasm and encouragement have been a driving force in our commitment to creating a valuable resource.

- Family and Friends: To our families and friends for their unwavering support, patience, and understanding during the long hours spent crafting this book. Your belief in us has been a constant source of motivation.

- Publishing Team: To the publishing team, editors, and professionals who helped shape and refine this manuscript. Your expertise and dedication have transformed ideas into a coherent narrative.

- The Creative Community: To the entire creative community, both established and emerging, for your boundless creativity and passion. You inspire us every day.

Remember that creativity is a collaborative endeavor, and your contributions to the world of art and entrepreneurship are invaluable. We hope this book serves as a source of knowledge, inspiration, and empowerment for all creative entrepreneurs on their remarkable journeys.

With heartfelt gratitude,

[**Simeon Favour**]

www.ingramcontent.com/pod-product-compliance
Lightning Source LLC
Chambersburg PA
CBHW071608270726
48661CB00019B/1659